HEALING
THE WOMAN'S
Soul

AN INTERACTIVE STUDY FOR WOMEN

TONYA H. WARE

ARCHWAY
PUBLISHING

Archway Publishing books may be ordered through booksellers or by contacting:

Archway Publishing
1663 Liberty Drive
Bloomington, IN 47403
www.archwaypublishing.com
844-669-3957

Because of the dynamic nature of the Internet, any web addresses or links contained in this book may have changed since publication and may no longer be valid. The views expressed in this work are solely those of the author and do not necessarily reflect the views of the publisher, and the publisher hereby disclaims any responsibility for them.

Any people depicted in stock imagery provided by Getty Images are models, and such images are being used for illustrative purposes only. Certain stock imagery © Getty Images.

ISBN: 978-1-6657-1789-2 (sc)
ISBN: 978-1-6657-1788-5 (hc)
ISBN: 978-1-6657-1787-8 (e)

Library of Congress Control Number: 2022900992

Print information available on the last page.

Archway Publishing rev. date: 4/27/2022

Contents

Your journey to wholeness begins …

On your journey to wholeness, enjoy the process!

Beloved, I wish above all things that thou mayest prosper
and be in health, even as thy **soul** prospereth.
—3 John 2 (KJV)

Meditate on This!

We prosper in life equal to our soul's prosperity.

Acknowledgments

I want to thank my love, Adrian Ware, for his continual support. To Mom Hairston, thank you for graciously sharing your life lessons with me so I could develop and grow into a strong woman. To the women who helped expand my study on this topic and those who attend the R.E.D. Women's Small Group, thank you for the great sessions and dialogue. A special thank-you goes to everyone who helped me bring this book to life.

Lastly, to my beautiful daughters, Wisdom Noelle and Wealth Joy, may you watch my evolving example and live your life healed, whole, prosperous, and fulfilled. Thank you for giving me a reason to be healed in my soul. You two are my greatest joy and achievement.

To everyone who will read this book and share it with a friend, thank you for allowing me to be a part of your journey to wholeness.

Introduction

I remember sitting and talking with my mom years ago. Mom Hairston told me a fascinating story about a time when she was a newlywed and young mother. One day, she looked outside and saw the postman dropping off mail in her box. As she started to walk outside to collect the mail, this enormous fear came over her, and she could not convince herself to go outside. Mom said the experience shocked her, and she wondered what made her have this fear.

Whenever my mother did not understand something in her life, she would get quiet and pray for clarity. As she prayed about this fear that kept her from going to her mailbox, she said something like a big TV screen appeared in her mind. On this screen, she saw herself as a preteen girl, walking home from school.

She lived close to a local neighbor who was elderly, so she thought it would be a kind gesture to stop on her way home from school and get this neighbor's mail. She approached the neighbor's house and stopped at the mailbox.

As she reached her hand in to get the lady's mail, she heard her neighbor scream, "Somebody help! Susan is stealing my mail!"

Mom said she dropped the mail and ran as fast as she could until she made it all the way home. Years passed, and my mother grew up, graduated from high school, met my father, and married. Seemingly, all of a sudden, she began having this overwhelming fear that was so great that she was afraid to go to her mailbox to get her mail. She realized that the traumatic experience she'd had as a young girl of the lady thinking she was stealing when she was trying to show kindness caused a crack in her soul that showed up later in life in the form of fear.

Every woman has experienced things in life that have shaped and molded her. Some things get into one's soul, causing feelings of fear, dread, and sadness. These feelings can eat away at one's peace. The hope is that this book will help women examine their souls. As women, we can choose to be healed and whole. As you read this book and engage in the interactive study assignments, get ready to develop a deeper understanding of your soul and what you can do to live your life to the fullest!

It is time to *heal* from past hurts, *discover* pathways to freedom, and *live* like days of heaven on earth.

One

THE BEGINNING

To study the woman's soul, I would like to take you on a journey that begins with the creation of all humanity. The story of the soul begins in Genesis 2.

> Heaven and earth were finished, down to the last detail. By the seventh day, God had finished his work. On the seventh day he rested from all his work. God blessed the seventh day. He made it a Holy Day because on that day he rested from his work, all the creating God had done. This is the story of how it all started, of Heaven and Earth when they were created. (Genesis 2:1–4 MSG)

> At the time God made Earth and Heaven, before any grasses or shrubs had sprouted from the ground— God hadn't yet sent rain on earth, nor was there anyone around to work the ground (the whole earth was watered by underground springs)—God formed Man out of dirt from the ground and blew into his nostrils the breath of life. *The Man came alive—a living soul!* In the original (Genesis 2:5–7 MSG)

> God took the Man and set him down in the Garden of Eden to work the ground and keep it in order. (Genesis 2:15 MSG)

> God put the Man into a deep sleep. As he slept, he removed one of his ribs and replaced it with flesh. *God then used the rib* that he had taken from the Man *to make woman* and presented her to the Man. (Genesis 2:21–22 MSG)

Note: The woman was the only creature presented to man. This is a significant clue. As women, we are so valuable, precious, powerful, and worthy that God presented us.

The Man said, "Finally! Bone of my bone, flesh of my flesh! Name her woman for she was made from Man." Therefore a man leaves his father and mother and embraces his wife. They become one flesh. The two of them, the Man and his Wife, were naked, but they felt no shame. (Genesis 2:23–25 MSG)

There are five significant keynotes from these scriptures.

KEYNOTE 1: THE SOUL CAME FROM GOD

Genesis 2:5–7 reveals that God formed man out of dirt from the ground and blew the breath of life into his nostrils. The man came alive—a living soul, a speaking spirit.

Since God is the Creator of all living things and his gifts are good, the soul is good in its created state. When God gave us souls, we became speaking spirits. Have you ever thought about how God created you as a living soul, as a speaking spirit? What do you think about this truth?

_____

_____

_____

_____

_____

_____

We are created with the power to speak into existence the kind of lives we desire. I remember learning this truth. When I realized that God had created me with a "good" soul, the way I saw myself changed. As I encounter things that come to injure, break, or crush my soul, I use my words, the part of me that is a speaking spirit, to overcome the challenges and attacks.

You are a living soul—a speaking spirit! What will you speak into existence?

_____

_____

_____

_____

_____

_____

_____

KEYNOTE 2: THE CONTENTS OF OUR SOULS IMPACT HOW WE LIVE

All our lives' moments—the happy memories we make, the things we meditate on, the conversations we have, and the trauma we experience—contribute to what lives in our souls. Think of your soul as a grocery cart. When you walk through the store, you can choose to put things in the basket. Some items you think about as you walk around the store and decide you don't want them before you get to the checkout counter.

Hurtful words or actions are frequently placed in our souls by people we love. But just like you can take things that you have decided you do not want out of your grocery basket, you can take things that you no longer want out of your soul. You can do this by following five steps.

1. Acknowledge all hurt to yourself and God.

   What hurts do you need to acknowledge?

   _____

   _____

   _____

   _____

   _____

   _____

   _____

2. Ask God to heal you. Trust that he will. Here is a prayer you can pray:

   > Father, you saw me while I was being formed in my mother's womb. I am wonderfully made. I am your handiwork, re-created in Christ Jesus. According to 1 Peter 2:24, you give me beauty for ashes, the oil of joy for mourning, and the garment of praise for the spirit of heaviness so that I might be a tree of righteousness and you might be glorified when I am healed. I say on the authority of your Word that I am redeemed. I have a joyful and confident hope

that you have healed me, and you will make me whole. Amen.

3. Choose words and actions that promote peace. Things you do not talk about will die.

    In what ways will you promote peace in your personal life?

    _____

    _____

    _____

    _____

    _____

    _____

    _____

    _____

    In what ways will you promote peace in your family?

    _____

    _____

    _____

    _____

    _____

In what ways will you promote peace in your community?

_____

_____

_____

_____

_____

4. Replace the things in your soul that you do not want by meditating on the Word of God.

TEN KEY SCRIPTURES FOR MEDITATION

I will meditate about your glory, splendor, majesty, and miracles. Your awe-inspiring deeds shall be on every tongue; I will proclaim your greatness. Everyone will tell about how good you are and sing about your righteousness. (Psalm 145:5–7 TLB)

Don't worry about anything; instead, pray about everything; tell God your needs, and don't forget to thank him for his answers. If you do this, you will experience God's peace, which is far more wonderful than the human mind can understand. His peace will keep your thoughts and your hearts quiet and at rest as you trust in Christ Jesus. (Philippians 4:6–7 TLB)

But blessed is the Man who trusts in the Lord and has made the Lord his hope and confidence. He is like a tree planted along a riverbank, with its roots reaching deep into the water—a tree not bothered by the heat nor worried by long months of drought. Its leaves stay green, and it goes right on producing all its luscious fruit. (Jeremiah 17:7–8 TLB)

I have been crucified with Christ: and I myself no longer live, but Christ lives in me. And the real-life I now have within this body is a result of my trusting in the Son of God, who loved me and gave himself for me. (Galatians 2:20 TLB)

But God is so rich in mercy; he loved us so much that even though we were spiritually dead and doomed by our sins, he gave us back our lives again when he raised Christ from the dead—only by His undeserved favor have we ever been saved. (Ephesians 2:4–5 TLB)

For the Lord your God has arrived to live among you. He is a mighty Savior. He will give you victory. He will rejoice over you with great gladness; he will love you and not accuse you." Is that a joyous choir I hear? No, it is the Lord himself exulting over you in happy song. (Zephaniah 3:17–18 TLB)

See how very much our heavenly father loves us, for he allows us to be called his children—think of it—and we really are! But since most people don't know God, naturally, they don't understand that we are his children. (1 John 3:1 TLB)

Yes, be bold and strong! Banish fear and doubt! For remember, the Lord your God is with you wherever you go. (Joshua 1:9 TLB)

His compassion never ends. It is only the Lord's mercies that have kept us from complete destruction. Great is his faithfulness; his loving-kindness begins afresh each day. (Lamentations 3:22–23 TLB)

God is bedrock under my feet, the castle in which I live, my rescuing knight. My God, where I run for dear life, hiding behind the boulders, safe in the granite hideout; My mountaintop refuge, he saves me from ruthless men. I sing to God the Praise-Lofty, and find myself safe and saved. (1 Samuel 22:3–4 MSG)

5.   Serve and encourage others as they overcome their challenges.
     In what ways will you serve others?

_____

_____

_____

_____

_____

KEYNOTE 3: THE SOUL HAS FIVE PARTS—
MIND, WILL, EMOTION, INTELLECT, AND IMAGINATION

When God gave us souls, he gave us all the parts of the soul to serve
us. Our minds were given to us so we could think of ways to live
empowered lives. Our wills were given to us so we could preserve,
be strong, and endure. Our emotions were given to us so we could
feel and have empathy and compassion. Our intellects were given
to us so we could be smart about decisions in life, develop answers,
and find solutions. Our imaginations were given to us so we could
dream and look forward to the future.

How is your mind serving you?

_____

_____

_____

_____

How is your will serving you?

_____

_____

_____

_____

_____

_____

_____

How are your emotions serving you?

_____

_____

_____

_____

_____

_____

_____

How is your intellect serving you?

_____

_____

_____

_____

_____

_____

How is your imagination serving you?

_____

_____

_____

_____

_____

_____

KEYNOTE 4: WHEN THE SOUL OPERATES AT ITS OPTIMUM LEVEL, THERE IS ORDER

In Genesis 2:15, God took the man and placed him down in the garden of Eden to work the ground and keep it in order.

Active people with healthy souls have rhythm and order in their lives. Order begins within the soul. When your thoughts and emotions are working for you and not against you, you are truly blessed. We must seek a life of order. We must clean up all messes and deal with incomplete issues so we can spend our days living, loving, creating, and advancing. Order does not come to restrict you. It comes to free up your attention so you can focus more on purpose and enjoying your life.

In what ways can you foster order in your life?

_____

_____

_____

_____

_____

_____

KEYNOTE 5: WHEN THE SOUL IS IN ONENESS WITH GOD, THERE IS NO SHAME.

Now this is excellent news! I speak to women all the time who are overwhelmed with shame and regret. I always tell them that in life, "We fall *up!*" Every problem, betrayal, abuse, wrong decision, mistake, misstep, and missed relationship can be used as an opportunity to grow, learn, and forgive; when a woman decides to forgive herself and cast off regret, joy overflows and peace increases. Just know, you deserve to be happy and healthy.

CHAPTER 1 SOUL CHECK-UP QUESTIONS:

1. Do you live like you have received God's breath?

_____

_____

_____

_____

_____

2. Have you recognized changes in the way you live based on what's in your soul?

_____

_____

_____

_____

_____

_____

3. Your soul is comprised of five parts. Are those parts working for you or against you?

_____

_____

_____

_____

_____

_____

_____

4. Does what you have in your soul bring order or chaos to your life?

_____

_____

_____

_____

_____

_____

5. Are you living in shame because of something in your soul?

_____

_____

_____

_____

_____

_____

_____

_____

THINK ON THIS!

In chapter 1 of this study on healing the woman's soul, we found this truth in Genesis 2:5–7 MSG.

At the time God made earth and heaven, before any grasses or shrubs had sprouted from the ground—God hadn't yet sent rain on earth, nor was there anyone around to work the ground (the whole earth was watered by underground springs)—God formed man out of dirt from the ground and blew into his nostrils the breath of life. The man came alive—a living soul, a speaking spirit.

Since you are *a living soul, a speaking spirit*, what will you say about yourself today?

I am:

_____

_____

_____

_____

_____

_____

I will:

_____

_____

_____

_____

_____

I can:

_____

_____

_____

_____

_____

_____

_____

I deserve:

_____

_____

_____

_____

_____

_____

_____

I believe:

_____

_____

_____

_____

_____

_____

_____

Beloved, I pray that in every way you may succeed
and prosper and be in good health [physically], just
as [I know] your **soul** prospers [spiritually].
—3 John 2 (AMP)

Meditate on This!

*When the soul is healed, a new level of
joy will manifest in your life.*

Two
THE FIRST BROKEN SOUL

In the early years of my marriage, I would list items I needed from the grocery store and give it to my husband. One day he came home after a few hours of shopping, but as I began taking items out of the bags, I noticed some things I'd requested were not in the there. Immediately, a wave of sadness came over me, and I begin to cry. My husband stood there, shocked and confused. He asked me a critical question: "What's the root of your tears?" As I prayed about it, God revealed the answer to me.

Growing up in a big family was so much fun. My parents had a noble profession. As pastors, they lived a life of service to others. What we did not have in money, we made up for in love. When it came to buying groceries, we mainly purchased foods that would keep us full. I would sit as a child and say to myself, *One day, when I grow up, I am going to eat whatever I want, whenever I want.* Yet, over the years, I developed a belief system that, no matter how much money I had, I would never be able to get what I truly wanted to eat. This belief manifested as deep sadness when I could not find what I desired in the grocery store. This incident sparked my curiosity about how experiences in life can cause an imprint—good or bad—on the soul.

We find the story of the first broken soul by studying the first woman, Eve.

GENESIS 3

> "The serpent was clever, more clever than any wild animal God had made. He spoke to the woman: 'Do I understand that God told you not to eat from any tree in the garden?' The woman said to the serpent, 'Not at all. We can eat from the trees in the garden. It's only about the tree in the middle of the garden that God said, "Don't eat from it; don't even touch it or you'll die.""" (Genesis 3:1–3 MSG)

KEYNOTE 1: THE SERPENT WAS NOT YET CURSED. SO THE SNAKE WAS UPRIGHT, AND ALL THE ANIMALS IN THE GARDEN LIVED IN HARMONY WITH ADAM AND EVE.

I think we must make a note of two things here.

1. Adam was meeting with God in the cool of the day. Eve relied on Adam to bring her into those conversations. Couples and families must have regular times to talk about God and study his Word.
2. Since the serpent was not cursed when he conversed with Eve, he did not look like a snake as we know them today. He appeared to her like a friend; she had no idea that she was about to make the biggest mistake of her life by listening to him.

> "The serpent told the woman, 'You won't die. God knows that the moment you eat from that tree, you'll see what's going on. You'll be just like God, knowing everything, ranging from good to evil.'" (Genesis 3:4–5 MSG)

KEYNOTE 2: A SIGN OF A BROKEN SOUL IS NOT BEING ABLE TO DISTINGUISH BETWEEN THE TRUTH AND A LIE.

Failing to tell the difference between good and evil can happen to any of us. But we can pray and ask God these things -

1. "Lord, don't let me be deceived. Block anything you do not want in my life."
2. "Lord, reveal yourself and give me the desire to follow your voice."

> "When the Woman saw that the tree looked like good eating and realized what she would get out of it

she'd know everything! She took and ate the fruit and then gave some to her husband, and he ate." (Genesis 3:6 MSG)

KEYNOTE 3: BEING RULED BY SENSES AND EMOTIONS IS ANOTHER SIGN OF A BROKEN SOUL.

We know that emotions are good because God made each of us with emotions. We get in trouble, though, when we allow emotions to rule us. The feeling itself is not the problem. What we do with our emotions is up to us. We must live by faith and not by feelings. We will always have feelings, but we should never allow them to be greater than our faith.

EMOTIONS AND YOUR RESPONSE

How do you respond when you feel the following emotions?

Grief:

_____

_____

_____

_____

_____

_____

Inspiration:

_____

_____

_____

_____

Fear:

_____

_____

_____

_____

Anger:

_____

_____

_____

_____

Sadness:

_____

_____

_____

_____

_____

Happiness:

_____

_____

_____

_____

_____

"Immediately the two of them did "see what's going on"- (they) saw themselves naked! They sewed fig leaves together as makeshift clothes for themselves. When they heard the sound of God strolling in the garden in the evening breeze, the Man and his Wife hid in the trees of the garden, hid from God." (Genesis 3:7–8 MSG)

KEYNOTE 4: OFTEN, A SIGN OF A BROKEN SOUL IS THE SPIRIT OF SHAME.

We all make mistakes, but if you live in continual shame, there is a place in your soul that longs to be healed. Shame is a jail keeper.

Shame can live inside the soul when certain things happen to us. But we do not have to live a life of shame. There is no condemnation and no shame in Christ. The more we meditate on the right things, the more we evict shame from our souls.

A PRAYER TO OVERCOME SHAME

> Heavenly Father, I give thanks that You created me. I ask that you free me from feelings of shame. I forgive myself and will no longer isolate myself from healthy, loving relationships, joyful experiences, and wholesome memories. Every time I feel shame, I will get quiet and call on your name. Help me to focus my thoughts on truth and not react to my feelings. I am forever grateful that You love and care for me. Amen.

"God called to the Man: 'Where are you?' He said, 'I heard you in the garden, and I was afraid because I was naked. And I hid.' God said, 'Who told you that you were naked? Did you eat from that tree I told you not to eat from?' The Man said, 'The Woman you gave me as a companion, she gave me fruit from the tree, and, yes, I ate it.'" (Genesis 3:9–12 MSG)

KEYNOTE 5: BLAMING PEOPLE OR SITUATIONS WHEN SOMETHING GOES WRONG IN OUR LIVES IS A SIGN OF A BROKEN SOUL. SHAME AND BLAME GO HAND IN HAND.

You can always tell when a person shows signs of a healthy soul; they no longer blame others for their situation. Even when wronged, it is crucial to believe that nothing can hold you back from a happy life. Once you take charge of your life, nothing can stop you from manifesting your unique greatness!

"God said to the woman, 'What is this that you've done?' 'The serpent seduced me,' she said, 'and I ate.'" (Genesis 3:12–13 MSG)

KEYNOTE 6: ANOTHER SIGN OF A BROKEN SOUL IS BEING EASILY SEDUCED IN THE AREAS OF SEX, FINANCES, AND RELATIONSHIPS.

It is easy to deceive, mislead, and manipulate a person who has a broken soul. We see this with Eve. Had Eve invited herself to the meetings God had with Adam, she would have been more confident in her worth and her status. But she was vulnerable, and when the serpent spoke to her, she became his easy prey.

This part of your interactive study is essential. When you complete this next assignment, you will be able to see a pattern and then avoid missteps, future abuse, and unnecessary trial and error in your life.

When you think back over your life, why do you think it has been so easy for you to be taken advantage of, deceived, or mistreated?

_____

_____

_____

_____

_____

"God told the serpent: 'Because you've done this, you're cursed, cursed beyond all cattle and wild animals, Cursed to slink on your belly and eat dirt all your life. I'm declaring war between you and the woman, between your offspring and hers. He'll wound your head, you'll wound his heel.'

"He told the woman: 'I'll multiply your pains in childbirth;

you'll give birth to your babies in pain. You'll want to please your husband, but he'll Lord it over you.'

"He told the Man: 'Because you listened to your wife and ate from the tree That I commanded you not to eat from, "Don't eat from this tree," The very ground is cursed because of you; getting food from the ground will be as painful as having babies is for your wife; you'll be working in pain all your life long. The ground will sprout thorns and weeds, you'll get your food the hard way, planting and tilling and harvesting, sweating in the fields from dawn to dusk, until you return to that ground yourself, dead and buried; you started as dirt, you'll end up dirt.'

"The Man, known as Adam, named his wife Eve because she was the mother of all the living. God made leather clothing for Adam and his wife and dressed them. God said, "The Man has become like one of us, capable of knowing everything, ranging from good to evil. What if he now should reach out and take fruit from the Tree-of- Life and eat, and live forever? Never—this cannot happen!

"So God expelled them from the Garden of Eden and sent them to work the ground, the same dirt out of which they'd been made. He threw them out of the garden and stationed angel-cherubim and a revolving sword of fire east of it, guarding the path to the Tree-of- Life." (Genesis 3:14–24 MSG)

KEYNOTE 7: A SIGN OF A BROKEN SOUL IS LIVING A LIFE OF SELF-INFLICTED STRUGGLE.

Self-inflicted pain happens all the time. Our decisions either bring us into effortless living, or they get us into a state of struggle. Had Eve fully connected to her relationship with God, she would have never been in a conversation with the serpent. The serpent, with his cunning ways, encouraged Eve to trade her birthright for a lie. Eve and Adam are expelled from their place of blessing, the garden. Their life after the garden was filled with pain, suffering, shortage, lack, jealousy, murder, and death.

CHAPTER 2 SOUL CHECK-UP QUESTIONS:

1. When you receive information, can you discern if it is true or false? *Explain.*

_____

_____

_____

_____

_____

_____

2. Are you ruled by your senses and emotions? *When?*

_____

_____

_____

_____

_____

_____

_____

3. Are you living in secret shame? *Be honest here.*

_____

_____

_____

_____

_____

_____

_____

4. Do you tend to blame others when things do not go your way? *Why?*

_____

_____

_____

_____

_____

_____

_____

5. Are you easily seduced? *How does it make you feel?*

_____

_____

_____

_____

_____

_____

_____

6. Do you find yourself experiencing self-inflicted struggles? *Why do you think this happens?*

_____

_____

_____

_____

_____

_____

_____

THINK ON THIS!

In chapter 2 of this study on healing the woman's soul, we found this truth in Genesis 3:1–3: The serpent was clever, more clever than any wild animal God had made. He spoke directly to the woman. However, had Eve leaned into her relationship with God, she would have recognized the trick the serpent was playing on her.

Are you developing your relationship with God?

_____

_____

_____

_____

_____

When God speaks to you, do you know his voice? Do you obey your intuition?

_____

_____

_____

_____

_____

Beloved, I pray that all may go well with you and that you
may be in good health, as it goes well with your **soul**.
—3 John 2 (ESV)

Meditate on This!

When healed in your soul, you will experience
freedom from the bondage that holds you captive.

Three

THE BENEFIT OF A
HEALED SOUL

My daughter Wisdom loves school. She would blow a kiss to me when I dropped her off when she was young. I loved hearing her sweet little voice say, "See you later, Momma." One day while on the playground, she did not realize she was standing in a bed of Mississippi fire ants, and they crawled all over her. In an instant, she was being bitten all over her little body. She screamed in terror. The incident was so traumatizing to her that she decided at six years old that she would never go outside again.

When her dad surprised her with her first bicycle, she looked up at him and said, "Daddy, move this furniture so I can ride my bike!" He tried for many months to convince her to get over her fear and go outside.

Fortunately, Wisdom had a kindergarten teacher named Mrs. Valentine. Each day, Mrs. Valentine brought Wisdom close and prayed with her. Then she would tell her that she would be right there if she needed her. Mrs. Valentine told Wisdom that she knew that the joy she would feel playing outside would be greater than the fear she felt about going outside. Eventually, Wisdom overcame the fear with this loving support.

For this chapter of *Healing the Soul of the Woman*, our focus will be on the benefits of a healed soul.

1 John 2 says, "Beloved, I wish above all things that thou mayest prosper (to help on the road, succeed in reaching; to succeed in business affairs) and be in health, even as thy soul (breath, spirit,) prospereth."

KEYNOTE 1: THE WOMAN'S SOUL MUST HEAL SO THAT SHE CAN HELP SOMEONE ELSE ON THEIR LIFE'S JOURNEY.

Name three people in your life you can help and how. *Remember, you should only help those who ask for or want your help. Providing this help should be a peaceful and fulfilling interaction.*

1. _____

   _____

   _____

   _____

   _____

2. _____

   _____

   _____

   _____

   _____

3. _____

   _____

   _____

   _____

   _____

KEYNOTE 2: THE WOMAN'S SOUL MUST HEAL SO SHE CAN SUCCEED IN REACHING HER GOD-GIVEN DESTINY.

Share three primary goals you want to accomplish this year.

1. _____

_____

_____

_____

2. _____

_____

_____

_____

3. _____

_____

_____

_____

KEYNOTE 3: THE WOMAN'S SOUL MUST HEAL TO HAVE BREATH (LIFE AND HEALTH) AND A FLOURISHING SPIRIT.

Share three ways you want to see your spirit flourish.

1. _____

   _____

   _____

   _____

   _____

2. _____

   _____

   _____

   _____

   _____

3. _____

   _____

   _____

   _____

   _____

CHAPTER 3 SOUL CHECK-UP QUESTIONS:

1. Is there something in your soul keeping you from making God a priority?

_____

_____

_____

_____

2. Is there something in your soul hindering your success?

_____

_____

_____

_____

3. Are there thoughts you are meditating on that are harming your health or your spirit?

_____

_____

_____

_____

THINK ON THIS!

The spirit, soul, and body of the woman are created to be even—meaning that we are supposed to live our lives being healthy physically, emotionally, financially, and spiritually—all at the *same* time. That's the goal. We must separate ourselves from the narrative that something will always go wrong or live in fear that something terrible is going to happen.

Since our prosperity in life is directly linked to the health of our souls, women must hone in on this truth.

AFFIRMATIONS FOR A HEALTHY SOUL

- I am worthy of what I desire.
- I possess what I need to be successful.
- I appreciate all the good things in my life.
- I am open to increased wealth.
- I am limitless, and anything is possible.
- I achieve whatever I set my mind to.
- I am consistent, intelligent, capable, and gifted.
- I believe I can.

I pray for good fortune in everything you do, and for your good
health—that your everyday affairs prosper, as well as your soul!
—3 John 2 (MSG)

Meditate on This!

The goal is to be healthy in the spirit, soul,
and body at the same time.

Four

A HEALED SOUL

I remember listening to a sermon, and the speaker commented that, in life, we as humans go through so much trauma and pain that we would one day go to heaven still carrying the results of the trauma. I thought to myself, *What a miserable existence.*

Although we as women face challenges, have issues, are sometimes heartbroken, and deal with pain, I don't think it has to define us. I believe we can be so aware of our souls that we will recognize when things come to crack us, and we can do the continual work needed to live healed. Let's talk about living with a healed soul.

"Now set your heart and your soul to seek the Lord your God; **arise therefore, and build** ye the sanctuary of the Lord God, to bring the ark of the covenant of the Lord, and the holy vessels of God, into the house that is to be built to the name of the Lord." (1 Chronicles 22:19 KJV)

Look at this exact text more in-depth.

"Now set your heart and soul to seek (**inquire of, require as your vital necessity**) the Lord your God. Arise and build the sanctuary of the Lord God, so that you may bring the ark of the covenant of the Lord and the holy articles and utensils of God into the house built for the Name (Presence) of the Lord." (1 Chronicles 22:19 AMP)

"Now give your heart and soul to the Lord your God, and do what he says. Build the holy place of the Lord God. Then bring the Box of the Lord's Agreement and **all the other holy things into the Temple built for the Lord's name.**" (1 Chronicles 22:19 Easy-to-Read Version)

KEYNOTE 1: FOR THE WOMAN'S SOUL TO HEAL AND REMAIN HEALED, A WORK OF SURRENDER MUST FIRST HAPPEN IN THE HEART.

Do you have something in your heart that you need to surrender to God? *Write it here; begin the process.*

_____

_____

_____

_____

KEYNOTE 2: ONCE A WOMAN HAS GIVEN HER HEART TO GOD BY SUBMITTING HER SPIRIT TO HIS WILL, SHE MUST THEN GIVE HER SOUL (MIND, WILL, EMOTIONS, INTELLECT, AND IMAGINATION) BACK TO GOD BY ACKNOWLEDGING AND OBEYING HIM IN ALL AREAS OF HER LIFE.

Share three areas where you need to submit your will to God. Name the areas where you have tried to fix things. Are you willing to give it to God and take your hands off the situation for good?

1. _____

_____

_____

_____

_____

2. _____

_____

_____

_____

_____

_____

_____

_____

3. _____

_____

_____

_____

_____

_____

_____

_____

KEYNOTE 3: A WOMAN WHO GIVES HER HEART TO GOD BY SEEKING HIS WISDOM WILL BE ABLE TO MOVE TOWARD THE PROCESS OF ARISING AND BUILDING HER HOUSE (BUILDING HER LIFE) IN LINE WITH GOD'S APPROVED PATTERN.

Name three people you can connect with (*and why you chose them*) that should mentor, train, or support you as you move toward your place of wholeness.

1. _____

_____

_____

_____

2. _____

_____

_____

_____

3. _____

_____

_____

_____

KEYNOTE 4: WHEN THE WOMAN FOLLOWS GOD'S DESIGN IN ALL THINGS, HER HOME IS COMPLETE WITH ALL TYPES OF BEAUTIFUL THINGS AND ABUNDANT BLESSINGS.

Share something beautiful in your life.

_____

_____

_____

_____

_____

_____

_____

Share a blessing in your life.

_____

_____

_____

_____

_____

_____

_____

CHAPTER 4 SOUL CHECK-UP QUESTIONS

1. Have you given your heart (the whole of you) to God? *If so, in what ways?*

_____

_____

_____

_____

_____

_____

2. Do you acknowledge and follow God in every aspect of your life? *If so, how?*

_____

_____

_____

_____

_____

_____

3. Do you see God as the ultimate source for wisdom? *If so, in what way have you used God's wisdom recently?*

_____

_____

_____

_____

_____

_____

_____

_____

4. Whose pattern do you model when building your life? *Why?*

_____

_____

_____

_____

_____

_____

_____

_____

5. The benefits of a healed soul are beautiful things and blessings. *Share some of the beautiful things in your life at the moment.*

_____

_____

_____

_____

_____

THINK ON THIS!

"Now set your heart and soul to seek (inquire of, require as your vital necessity) the Lord your God. Arise and build the sanctuary of the Lord God, so that you may bring the ark of the covenant of the Lord and the holy articles and utensils of God into the house built for the Name (Presence) of the Lord." (1 Chronicles 22:19 AMP)

1. Women who want to live with a healed soul—inquire or ask for information from the Lord.

2. Women who want to live with a healed soul—exalt God's Word above all other wisdom.

3. Women who want to live with a healed soul—understand the value of building their faith through faith-filled connections.

4. Women who want to live with a healed soul—believe in and buy-in to God's dream for them.

5. Women who want to live with a healed soul—spend regular time in the presence of God.

Ultimately, you hold the key to your overall success in life. Success is a journey, and as you take one step at a time toward a healed soul, you will begin to enjoy life on a brand-new level!

Prayers for the Soul

A Prayer for Peaceful Sleep

Father God, I pray over every thought, every
imagination, and every dream.
I lay down and have sweet rest and peaceful sleep.
Thank you for the spirit of comfort that holds my
heart and causes me to enjoy days of ease.

As I sleep, counsel my heart and reveal to me your
purpose and plan. Thank you for your answers, new
strategies, favor, and open doors. My body
and soul rest confidently in you.
Amen.

A Prayer for Boldness

I am of good courage. I can come fearlessly, confidently,
and boldly to God's throne of grace and receive mercy,
find grace, and help in the time of my need.
I take comfort. I am encouraged, and I am joyful when I say,
"The Lord is my Helper, I will not be seized with alarm."
I will not fear or dread or be terrified. I am bold as a lion,
for I have been made the righteousness of God in
Christ. I am complete in Him!
Amen.

A Prayer for the Victorious Woman

Father, my hope and expectation are in You. I live an overcoming life. I live in daily expectation that I will live in abundance. Every need in my life is met. I have a sound mind. I live a long life because I am redeemed. I walk in divine health and healing.

My life is delivered from destruction; I overcome with my faith. My mind is alert; my body is strong. I live a life of purpose, and I am a blessing.
Amen.

A Prayer for Healing

Father, I confess Your Word concerning healing. I abide and remain stable and fixed under Your protection. I have the assurance of the angel of the Lord encamping around me. I ask that Your healing power flow through every cell of my being.

I recognize all stressful triggers that have hindered me from walking in health. I remove myself from all unhealthy behaviors. I trust in You to make me whole. I have health and healing now in the Name of Jesus.
Amen.

A Prayer of Healing for Damaged Emotions

Father, I admit I have felt shame and emotional hurt. You are my help and my healer. You surround me with songs of grace and comfort. I am Your handiwork. I will not fear, and I will not be ashamed. Neither will I be confused or depressed.

You give me beauty for ashes. I choose to forgive all who have wronged me in any way. You are my peace. I thank you that you will be with me always. You are my hope.
Amen.

Twenty-One Days to a Happy Soul

Do something every day
that brings you joy!

Mind your own business.

Stop and breathe deeply.
Then smile.

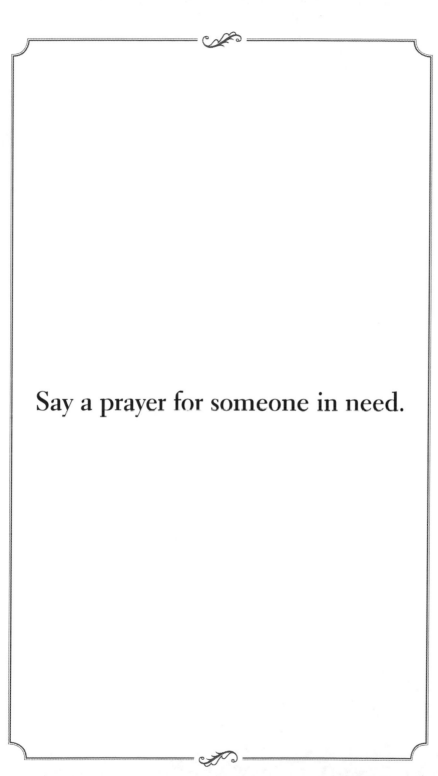

Say a prayer for someone in need.

Stay out of debt.

Laugh for no reason.

Don't complain. Be happy.

Invest in a child.

Forgive the past.

Don't rehearse hurt.

Accept grace.

Show mercy.

Let someone else decide.

Say yes.

Don't overthink things.

Don't make things bigger
than they arc.

Hug someone!

Accept love.

Give love.

Travel.

Become. Don't just talk
about it, be about it!

*Keep learning and growing until you
have a happy, healthy soul.*

Book Tonya Ware for Your Event
Author, Speaker, & Performer
Tonya H. Ware
TonyaHairstonWare@gmail.com
Events@TheSuccessHouse.CO
601.260.1848

Connect with Tonya Ware

Printed in the United States
by Baker & Taylor Publisher Services